COLOR IN THE STATE ONCE YOU COMPLETE YOUR RESEARCH ON THAT STATE

Draw/fill in the blanks

STATE CAPITAL: ______________________________

STATE FLAG

REGION

- ◯ Northeast
- ◯ Southwest
- ◯ West
- ◯ Midwest
- ◯ Southeast

STATE BIRD

____

STATE FLOWER

____

COLOR IN THE STATE ON THE MAP BELOW

ONE LANDMARK

AN INTERESTING FACT

NATURAL RESOURCES

Draw/fill in the blanks

STATE CAPITAL: ______________________

STATE FLAG

REGION

- ◯ Northeast
- ◯ Southwest
- ◯ West
- ◯ Midwest
- ◯ Southeast

STATE BIRD

____

STATE FLOWER

____

COLOR IN THE STATE ON THE MAP BELOW

ONE LANDMARK

AN INTERESTING FACT

NATURAL RESOURCES

Draw/fill in the blanks

STATE CAPITAL: ______________________________

STATE FLAG

REGION

- ◯ Northeast
- ◯ Southwest
- ◯ West
- ◯ Midwest
- ◯ Southeast

STATE BIRD

____

STATE FLOWER

____

COLOR IN THE STATE ON THE MAP BELOW

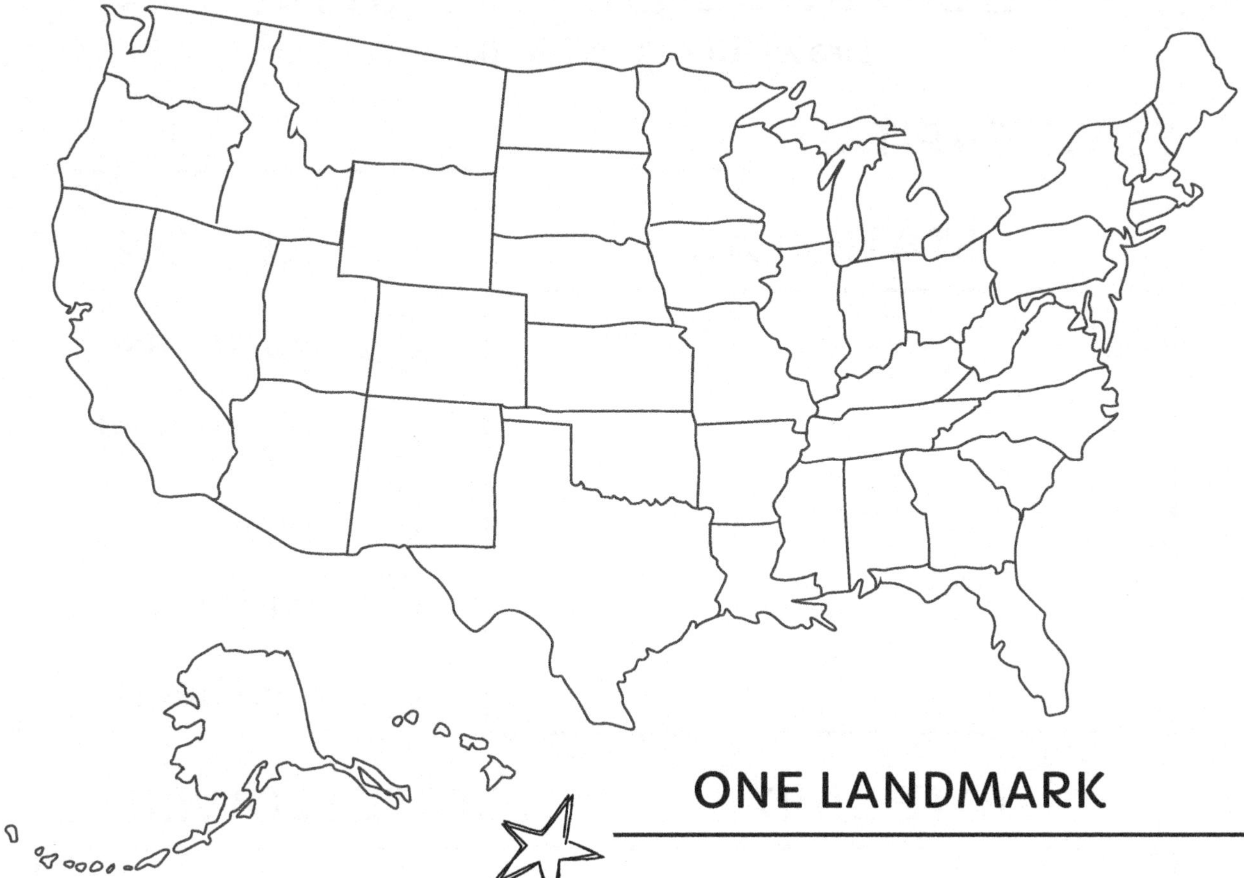

ONE LANDMARK

AN INTERESTING FACT

Draw/fill in the blanks

STATE CAPITAL: ______________________

STATE FLAG

REGION

- ◯ Northeast
- ◯ Southwest
- ◯ West
- ◯ Midwest
- ◯ Southeast

STATE BIRD

____

STATE FLOWER

____

COLOR IN THE STATE ON THE MAP BELOW

ONE LANDMARK

AN INTERESTING FACT

NATURAL RESOURCES

Draw/fill in the blanks

STATE CAPITAL: ______________________________

STATE FLAG

REGION

- ○ Northeast
- ○ Southwest
- ○ West
- ○ Midwest
- ○ Southeast

STATE BIRD

____

STATE FLOWER

____

COLOR IN THE STATE ON THE MAP BELOW

ONE LANDMARK

NATURAL RESOURCES

AN INTERESTING FACT

Draw/fill in the blanks

STATE CAPITAL: ______________________

STATE FLAG

REGION

- ◯ Northeast
- ◯ Southwest
- ◯ West
- ◯ Midwest
- ◯ Southeast

STATE BIRD

____

STATE FLOWER

____

COLOR IN THE STATE ON THE MAP BELOW

ONE LANDMARK

AN INTERESTING FACT

NATURAL RESOURCES

Draw/fill in the blanks

STATE CAPITAL: ______________________

STATE FLAG

REGION

- ◯ Northeast
- ◯ Southwest
- ◯ West
- ◯ Midwest
- ◯ Southeast

STATE BIRD

____

STATE FLOWER

____

COLOR IN THE STATE ON THE MAP BELOW

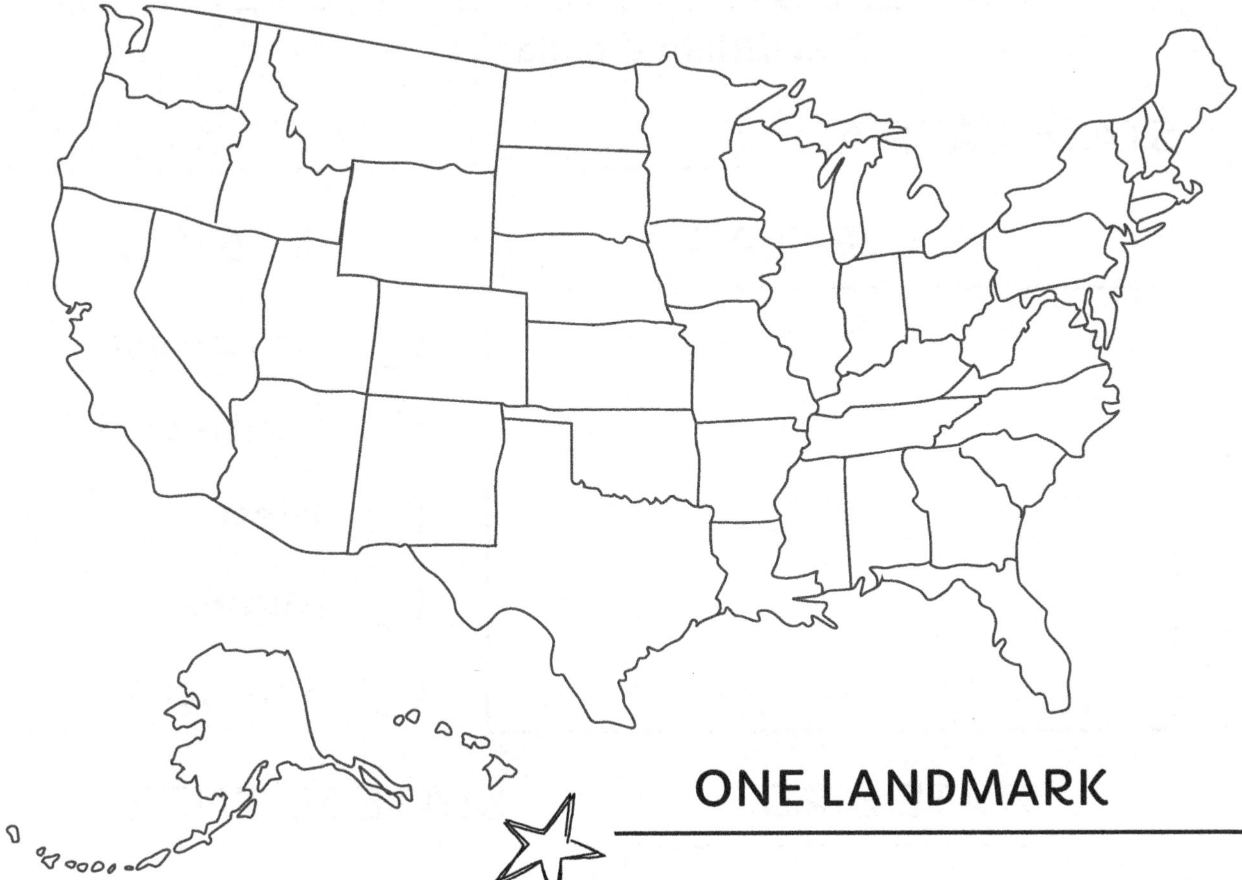

ONE LANDMARK

AN INTERESTING FACT

Draw/fill in the blanks

STATE CAPITAL: ______________________________

STATE FLAG

REGION

- ◯ Northeast
- ◯ Southwest
- ◯ West
- ◯ Midwest
- ◯ Southeast

STATE BIRD

____

STATE FLOWER

____

COLOR IN THE STATE ON THE MAP BELOW

ONE LANDMARK

AN INTERESTING FACT

NATURAL RESOURCES

Draw/fill in the blanks

STATE CAPITAL: ______________________

STATE FLAG

REGION

- ◯ Northeast
- ◯ Southwest
- ◯ West
- ◯ Midwest
- ◯ Southeast

STATE BIRD

____

STATE FLOWER

____

COLOR IN THE STATE ON THE MAP BELOW

ONE LANDMARK

AN INTERESTING FACT

NATURAL RESOURCES

Draw/fill in the blanks

STATE CAPITAL: ______________________

STATE FLAG

REGION

- ◯ Northeast
- ◯ Southwest
- ◯ West
- ◯ Midwest
- ◯ Southeast

STATE BIRD

____

STATE FLOWER

____

COLOR IN THE STATE ON THE MAP BELOW

ONE LANDMARK

AN INTERESTING FACT

NATURAL RESOURCES

Draw/fill in the blanks

STATE CAPITAL: ______________________________

STATE FLAG

REGION

- ◯ Northeast
- ◯ Southwest
- ◯ West
- ◯ Midwest
- ◯ Southeast

STATE BIRD

____

STATE FLOWER

____

COLOR IN THE STATE ON THE MAP BELOW

ONE LANDMARK

AN INTERESTING FACT

NATURAL RESOURCES

Draw/fill in the blanks

STATE CAPITAL: ______________________

STATE FLAG

REGION

- ◯ Northeast
- ◯ Southwest
- ◯ West
- ◯ Midwest
- ◯ Southeast

STATE BIRD

____

STATE FLOWER

____

COLOR IN THE STATE ON THE MAP BELOW

ONE LANDMARK

AN INTERESTING FACT

NATURAL RESOURCES

Draw/fill in the blanks

STATE CAPITAL: ________________________________

STATE FLAG

REGION

- ○ Northeast
- ○ Southwest
- ○ West
- ○ Midwest
- ○ Southeast

STATE BIRD

____

STATE FLOWER

____

COLOR IN THE STATE ON THE MAP BELOW

ONE LANDMARK

AN INTERESTING FACT

NATURAL RESOURCES

Draw/fill in the blanks

STATE CAPITAL: ______________________

STATE FLAG

REGION

- ○ Northeast
- ○ Southwest
- ○ West
- ○ Midwest
- ○ Southeast

STATE BIRD

____

STATE FLOWER

____

COLOR IN THE STATE ON THE MAP BELOW

ONE LANDMARK

AN INTERESTING FACT

NATURAL RESOURCES

Draw/fill in the blanks

STATE CAPITAL: ______________________

STATE FLAG

REGION

- ◯ Northeast
- ◯ Southwest
- ◯ West
- ◯ Midwest
- ◯ Southeast

STATE BIRD

____

STATE FLOWER

____

COLOR IN THE STATE ON THE MAP BELOW

ONE LANDMARK

AN INTERESTING FACT

NATURAL RESOURCES

Draw/fill in the blanks

STATE CAPITAL: ______________________

STATE FLAG

REGION

- ◯ Northeast
- ◯ Southwest
- ◯ West
- ◯ Midwest
- ◯ Southeast

STATE BIRD

____

STATE FLOWER

____

COLOR IN THE STATE ON THE MAP BELOW

ONE LANDMARK

AN INTERESTING FACT

NATURAL RESOURCES

Draw/fill in the blanks

STATE CAPITAL: ______________________________

STATE FLAG

REGION

- ○ Northeast
- ○ Southwest
- ○ West
- ○ Midwest
- ○ Southeast

STATE BIRD

____

STATE FLOWER

____

COLOR IN THE STATE ON THE MAP BELOW

ONE LANDMARK

AN INTERESTING FACT

NATURAL RESOURCES

Draw/fill in the blanks

STATE CAPITAL: ______________________

STATE FLAG

REGION

- ◯ Northeast
- ◯ Southwest
- ◯ West
- ◯ Midwest
- ◯ Southeast

STATE BIRD

____

STATE FLOWER

____

COLOR IN THE STATE ON THE MAP BELOW

ONE LANDMARK

AN INTERESTING FACT

NATURAL RESOURCES

Draw/fill in the blanks

STATE CAPITAL: ______________________________

STATE FLAG

REGION

- ◯ Northeast
- ◯ Southwest
- ◯ West
- ◯ Midwest
- ◯ Southeast

STATE BIRD

____

STATE FLOWER

____

COLOR IN THE STATE ON THE MAP BELOW

ONE LANDMARK

AN INTERESTING FACT

NATURAL RESOURCES

Draw/fill in the blanks

STATE CAPITAL: ______________________________

STATE FLAG

REGION

- ◯ Northeast
- ◯ Southwest
- ◯ West
- ◯ Midwest
- ◯ Southeast

STATE BIRD

____

STATE FLOWER

____

COLOR IN THE STATE ON THE MAP BELOW

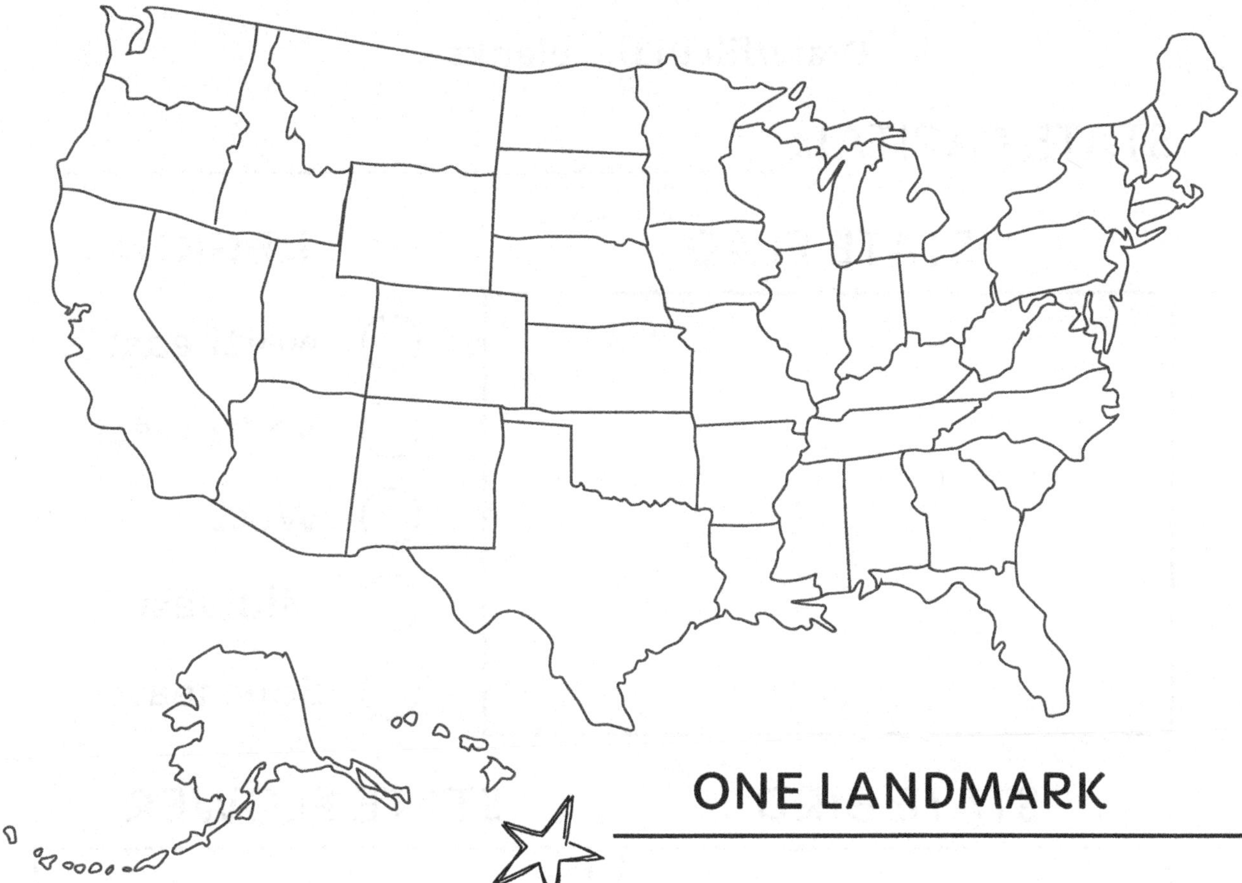

ONE LANDMARK

AN INTERESTING FACT

MASSACHUSETTS

Draw/fill in the blanks

STATE CAPITAL: ______________________________

STATE FLAG

REGION

- ◯ Northeast
- ◯ Southwest
- ◯ West
- ◯ Midwest
- ◯ Southeast

STATE BIRD

____

STATE FLOWER

____

COLOR IN THE STATE ON THE MAP BELOW

ONE LANDMARK

AN INTERESTING FACT

NATURAL RESOURCES

Draw/fill in the blanks

STATE CAPITAL: ______________________________

STATE FLAG

REGION

- ◯ Northeast
- ◯ Southwest
- ◯ West
- ◯ Midwest
- ◯ Southeast

STATE BIRD

____

STATE FLOWER

____

COLOR IN THE STATE ON THE MAP BELOW

ONE LANDMARK

AN INTERESTING FACT

NATURAL RESOURCES

Draw/fill in the blanks

STATE CAPITAL: ______________________________

STATE FLAG

REGION

- ◯ Northeast
- ◯ Southwest
- ◯ West
- ◯ Midwest
- ◯ Southeast

STATE BIRD

____

STATE FLOWER

____

COLOR IN THE STATE ON THE MAP BELOW

ONE LANDMARK

AN INTERESTING FACT

NATURAL RESOURCES

Draw/fill in the blanks

STATE CAPITAL: ______________________________

STATE FLAG

REGION

- ○ Northeast
- ○ Southwest
- ○ West
- ○ Midwest
- ○ Southeast

STATE BIRD

____

STATE FLOWER

____

COLOR IN THE STATE ON THE MAP BELOW

ONE LANDMARK

AN INTERESTING FACT

NATURAL RESOURCES

Draw/fill in the blanks

STATE CAPITAL: ______________________

STATE FLAG

REGION

- ○ Northeast
- ○ Southwest
- ○ West
- ○ Midwest
- ○ Southeast

STATE BIRD

____

STATE FLOWER

____

COLOR IN THE STATE ON THE MAP BELOW

ONE LANDMARK

AN INTERESTING FACT

NATURAL RESOURCES

Draw/fill in the blanks

STATE CAPITAL: ______________________

STATE FLAG

REGION

- ◯ Northeast
- ◯ Southwest
- ◯ West
- ◯ Midwest
- ◯ Southeast

STATE BIRD

____

STATE FLOWER

____

COLOR IN THE STATE ON THE MAP BELOW

ONE LANDMARK

AN INTERESTING FACT

NATURAL RESOURCES

Draw/fill in the blanks

STATE CAPITAL: ______________________________

STATE FLAG

REGION

- ◯ Northeast
- ◯ Southwest
- ◯ West
- ◯ Midwest
- ◯ Southeast

STATE BIRD

____

STATE FLOWER

____

COLOR IN THE STATE ON THE MAP BELOW

ONE LANDMARK

AN INTERESTING FACT

NATURAL RESOURCES

Draw/fill in the blanks

STATE CAPITAL: ______________________

STATE FLAG

REGION

- ◯ Northeast
- ◯ Southwest
- ◯ West
- ◯ Midwest
- ◯ Southeast

STATE BIRD

____

STATE FLOWER

____

COLOR IN THE STATE ON THE MAP BELOW

ONE LANDMARK

AN INTERESTING FACT

NATURAL RESOURCES

Draw/fill in the blanks

STATE CAPITAL: ______________________________

STATE FLAG

REGION

- ◯ Northeast
- ◯ Southwest
- ◯ West
- ◯ Midwest
- ◯ Southeast

STATE BIRD

____

STATE FLOWER

____

COLOR IN THE STATE ON THE MAP BELOW

ONE LANDMARK

AN INTERESTING FACT

NATURAL RESOURCES

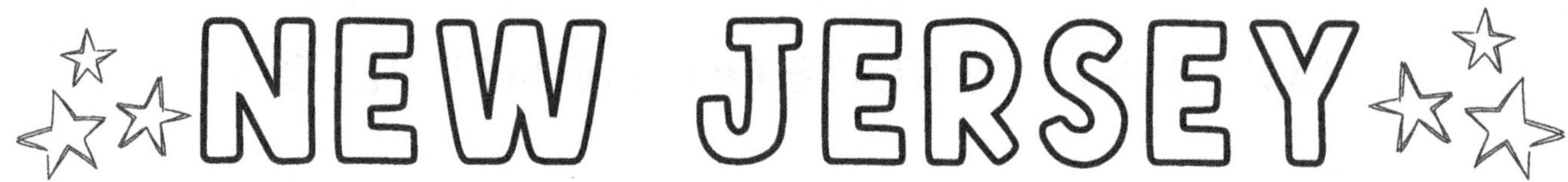

Draw/fill in the blanks

STATE CAPITAL: ______________________________

STATE FLAG

REGION

- ◯ Northeast
- ◯ Southwest
- ◯ West
- ◯ Midwest
- ◯ Southeast

STATE BIRD

____

STATE FLOWER

____

COLOR IN THE STATE ON THE MAP BELOW

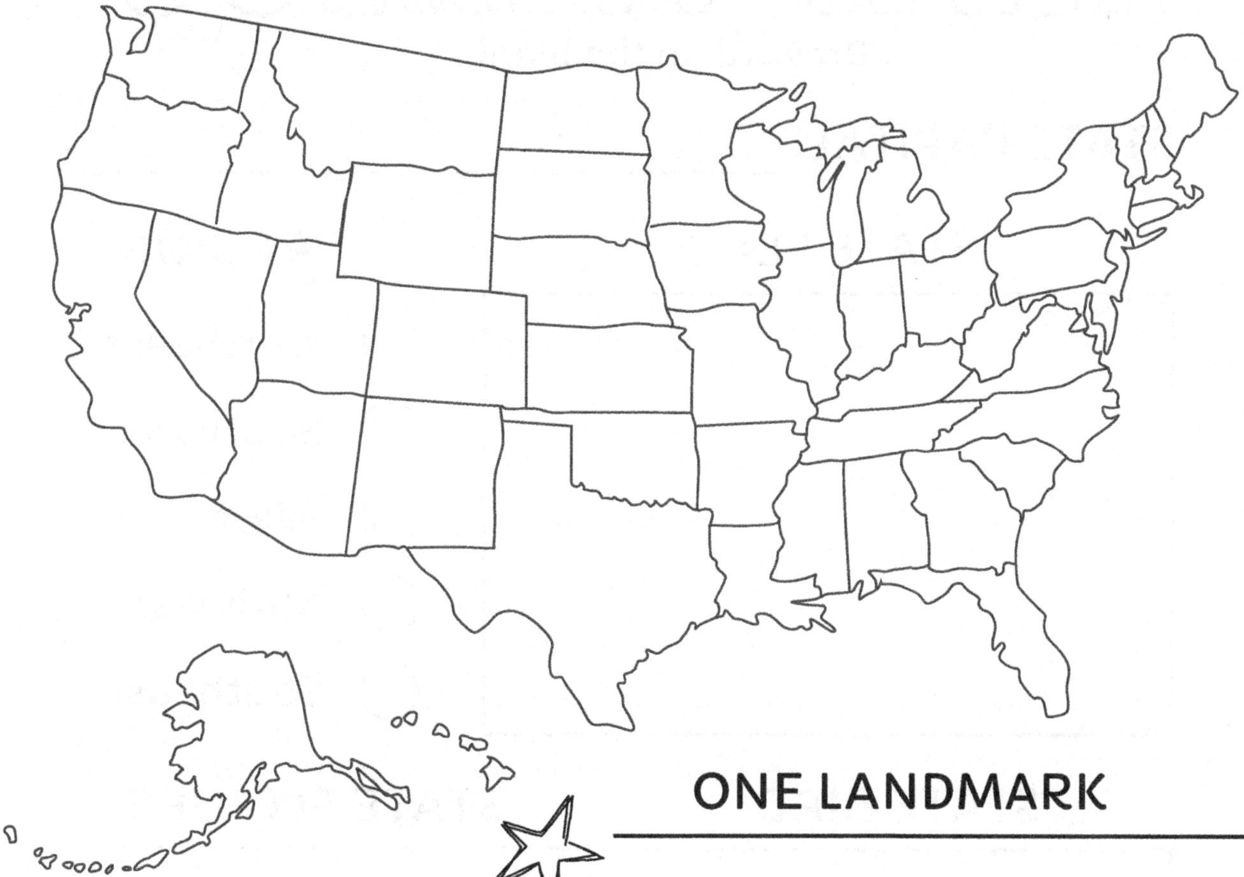

ONE LANDMARK

AN INTERESTING FACT

Draw/fill in the blanks

STATE CAPITAL: ______________________________

STATE FLAG

REGION

- ◯ Northeast
- ◯ Southwest
- ◯ West
- ◯ Midwest
- ◯ Southeast

STATE BIRD

____

STATE FLOWER

____

COLOR IN THE STATE ON THE MAP BELOW

ONE LANDMARK

AN INTERESTING FACT

NATURAL RESOURCES

Draw/fill in the blanks

STATE CAPITAL: ______________________

STATE FLAG

REGION

- ○ Northeast
- ○ Southwest
- ○ West
- ○ Midwest
- ○ Southeast

STATE BIRD

____

STATE FLOWER

____

COLOR IN THE STATE ON THE MAP BELOW

ONE LANDMARK

AN INTERESTING FACT

NATURAL RESOURCES

Draw/fill in the blanks

STATE CAPITAL: ____________________

STATE FLAG

REGION

- ◯ Northeast
- ◯ Southwest
- ◯ West
- ◯ Midwest
- ◯ Southeast

STATE BIRD

____

STATE FLOWER

____

COLOR IN THE STATE ON THE MAP BELOW

ONE LANDMARK

AN INTERESTING FACT

NATURAL RESOURCES

Draw/fill in the blanks

STATE CAPITAL: ______________________________

STATE FLAG

REGION

- ◯ Northeast
- ◯ Southwest
- ◯ West
- ◯ Midwest
- ◯ Southeast

STATE BIRD

____

STATE FLOWER

____

COLOR IN THE STATE ON THE MAP BELOW

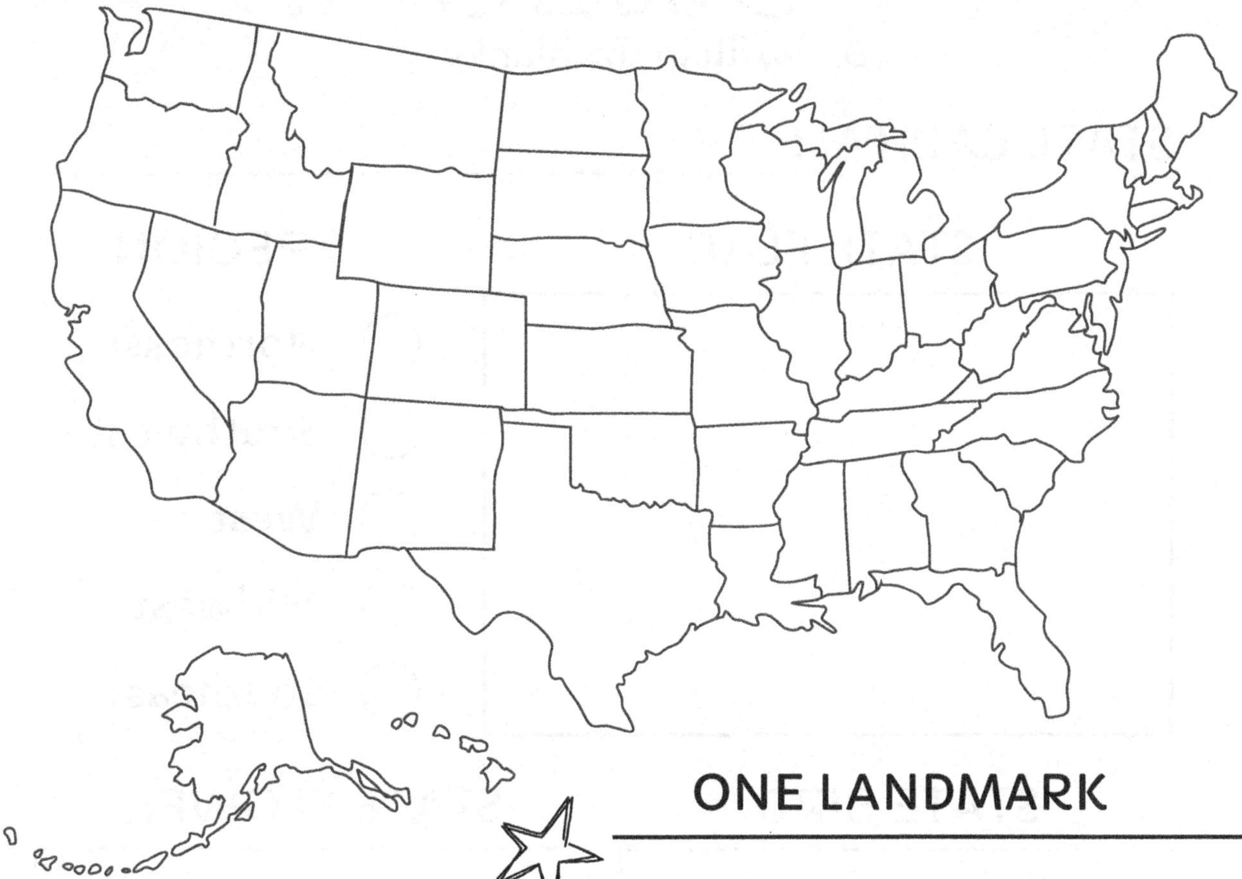

ONE LANDMARK

AN INTERESTING FACT

Draw/fill in the blanks

STATE CAPITAL: ______________________________

STATE FLAG

REGION

- ◯ Northeast
- ◯ Southwest
- ◯ West
- ◯ Midwest
- ◯ Southeast

STATE BIRD

____

STATE FLOWER

____

COLOR IN THE STATE ON THE MAP BELOW

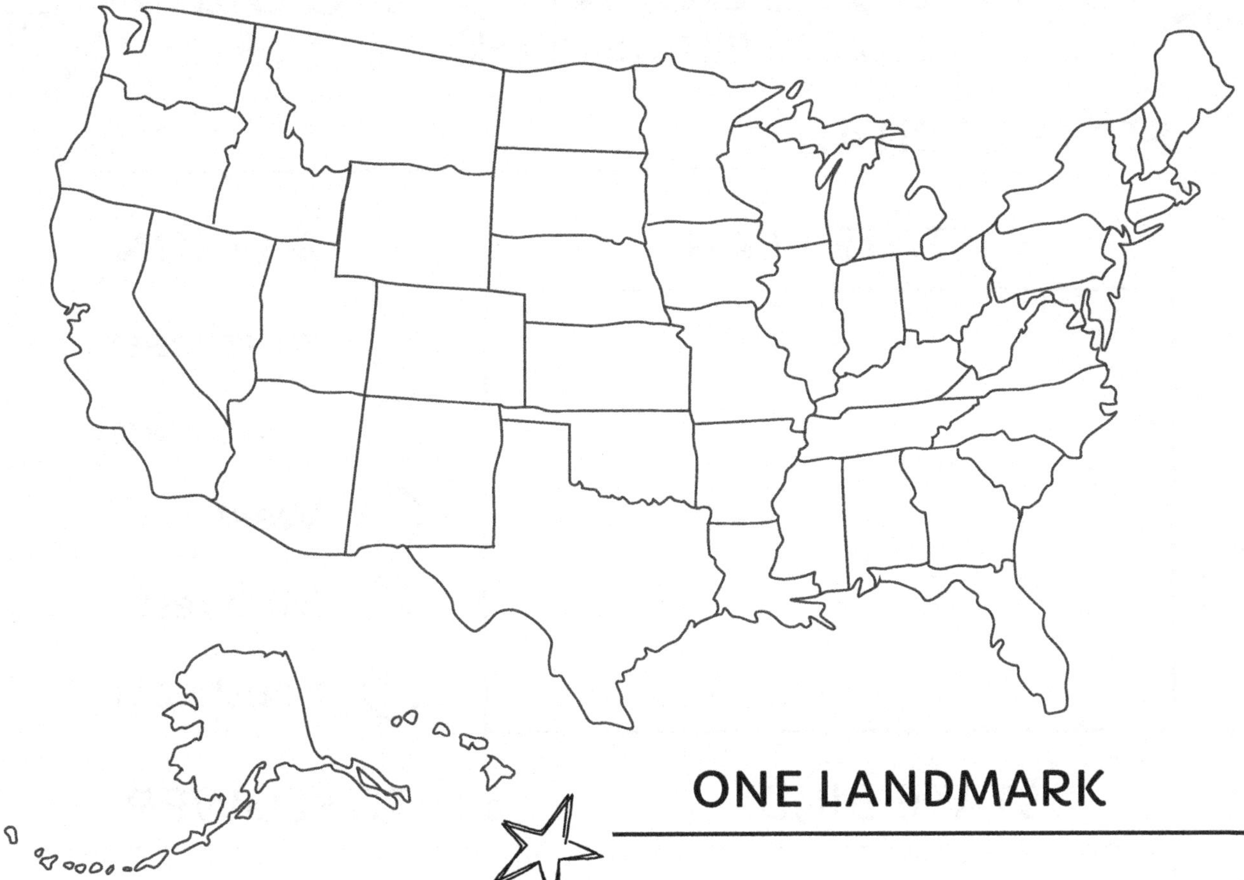

ONE LANDMARK

AN INTERESTING FACT

Draw/fill in the blanks

STATE CAPITAL: ______________________

STATE FLAG

REGION

- Northeast
- Southwest
- West
- Midwest
- Southeast

STATE BIRD

____

STATE FLOWER

____

COLOR IN THE STATE ON THE MAP BELOW

ONE LANDMARK

AN INTERESTING FACT

____

____

____

____

NATURAL RESOURCES

Draw/fill in the blanks

STATE CAPITAL: ______________________________

STATE FLAG

REGION

- ◯ Northeast
- ◯ Southwest
- ◯ West
- ◯ Midwest
- ◯ Southeast

STATE BIRD

____

STATE FLOWER

____

COLOR IN THE STATE ON THE MAP BELOW

ONE LANDMARK

AN INTERESTING FACT

NATURAL RESOURCES

Draw/fill in the blanks

STATE CAPITAL: ______________________________

STATE FLAG

REGION

- ◯ Northeast
- ◯ Southwest
- ◯ West
- ◯ Midwest
- ◯ Southeast

STATE BIRD

____

STATE FLOWER

____

COLOR IN THE STATE ON THE MAP BELOW

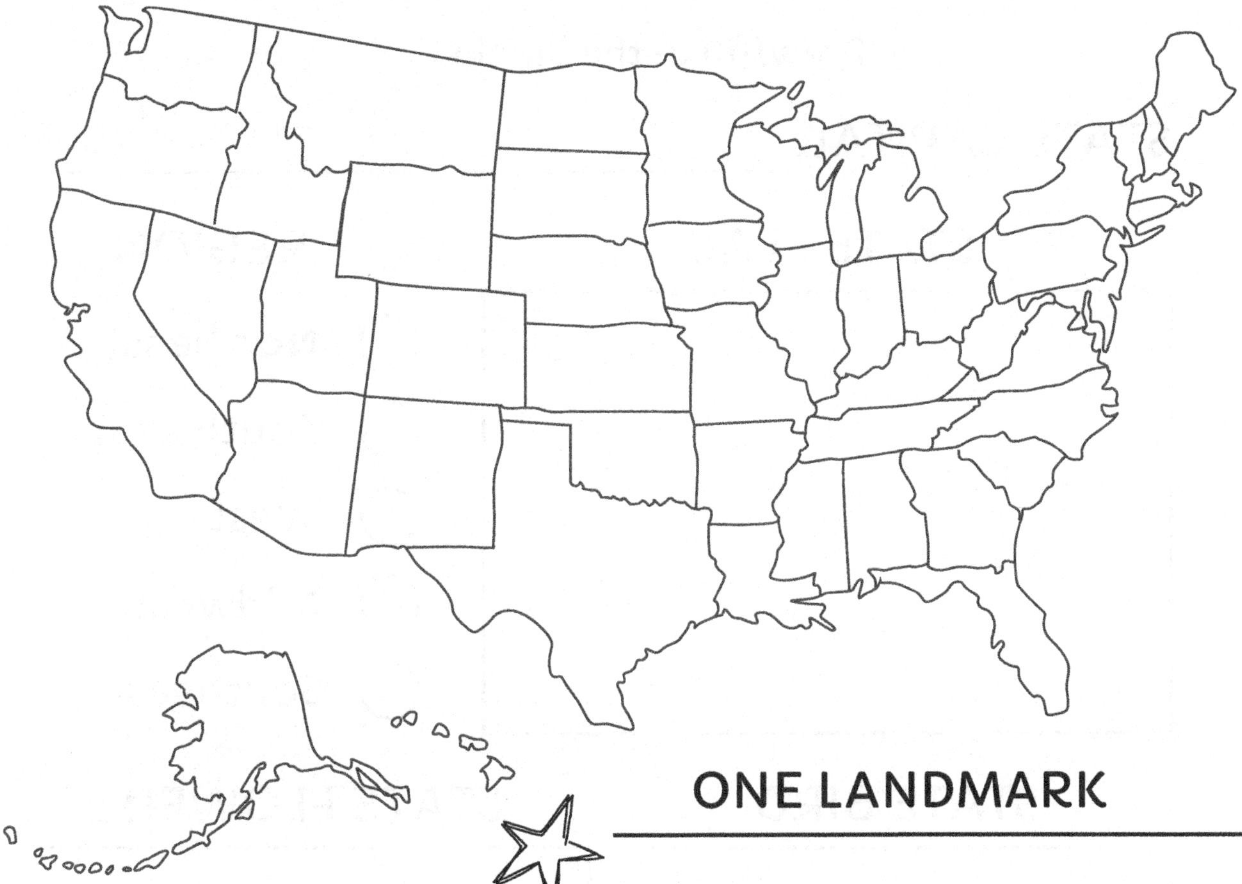

ONE LANDMARK

AN INTERESTING FACT

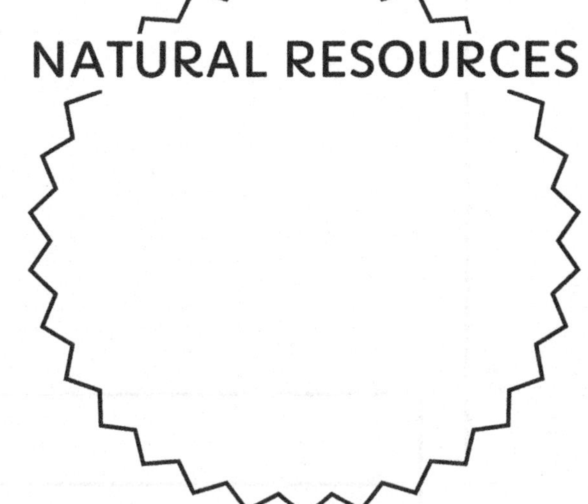

Draw/fill in the blanks

STATE CAPITAL: ______________________

STATE FLAG

REGION

- ◯ Northeast
- ◯ Southwest
- ◯ West
- ◯ Midwest
- ◯ Southeast

STATE BIRD

____

STATE FLOWER

____

COLOR IN THE STATE ON THE MAP BELOW

ONE LANDMARK

AN INTERESTING FACT

NATURAL RESOURCES

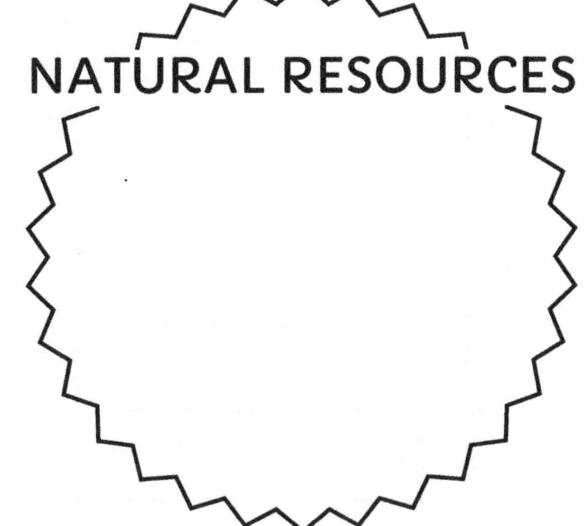

Draw/fill in the blanks

STATE CAPITAL: ______________________________

STATE FLAG

REGION

- ◯ Northeast
- ◯ Southwest
- ◯ West
- ◯ Midwest
- ◯ Southeast

STATE BIRD

____

STATE FLOWER

____

COLOR IN THE STATE ON THE MAP BELOW

ONE LANDMARK

AN INTERESTING FACT

NATURAL RESOURCES

Draw/fill in the blanks

STATE CAPITAL: ______________________

STATE FLAG

REGION

○ Northeast

○ Southwest

○ West

○ Midwest

○ Southeast

STATE BIRD

____

STATE FLOWER

____

COLOR IN THE STATE ON THE MAP BELOW

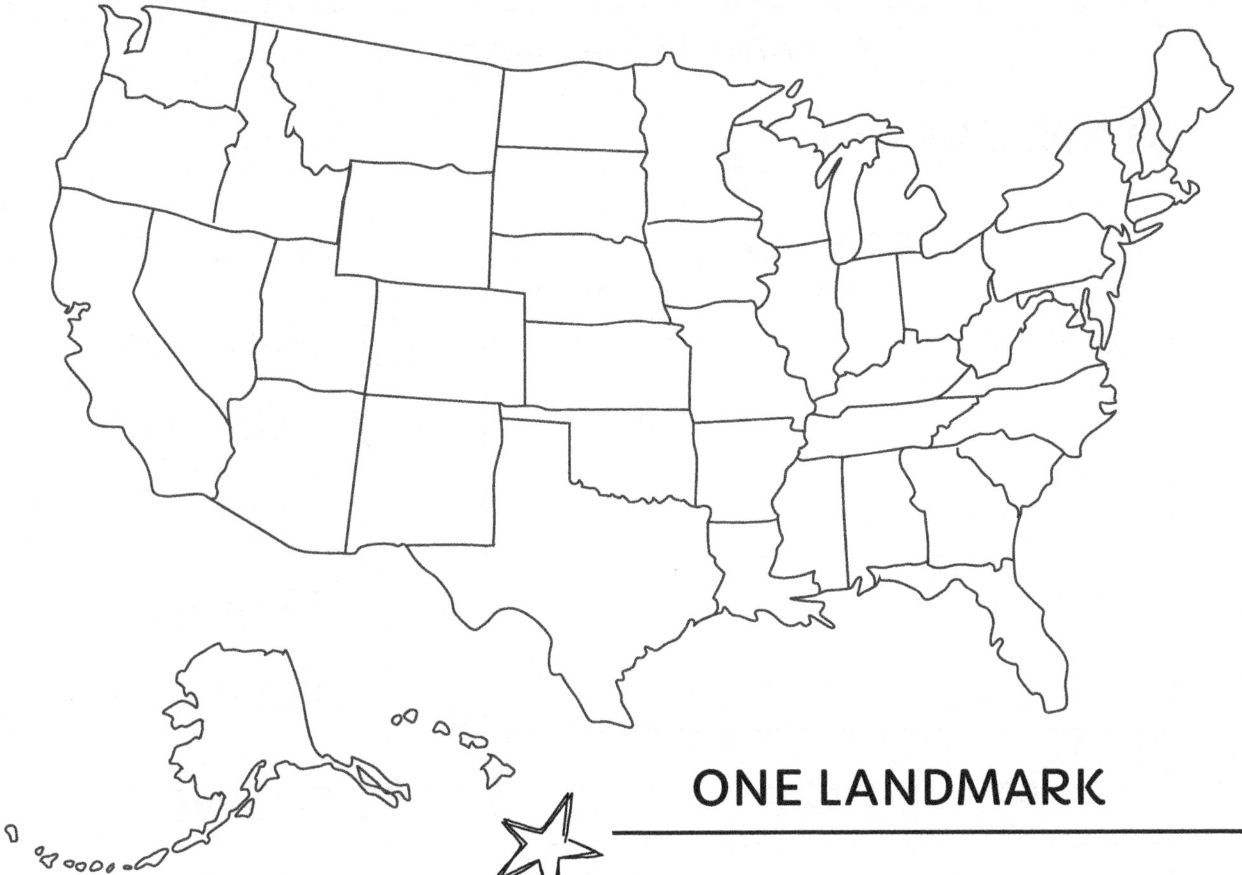

ONE LANDMARK

AN INTERESTING FACT

Draw/fill in the blanks

STATE CAPITAL: ______________________________

STATE FLAG

REGION

- ◯ Northeast
- ◯ Southwest
- ◯ West
- ◯ Midwest
- ◯ Southeast

STATE BIRD

____

STATE FLOWER

____

COLOR IN THE STATE ON THE MAP BELOW

ONE LANDMARK

AN INTERESTING FACT

NATURAL RESOURCES

Draw/fill in the blanks

STATE CAPITAL: ______________________________

STATE FLAG

REGION

- ◯ Northeast
- ◯ Southwest
- ◯ West
- ◯ Midwest
- ◯ Southeast

STATE BIRD

____

STATE FLOWER

____

COLOR IN THE STATE ON THE MAP BELOW

ONE LANDMARK

AN INTERESTING FACT

NATURAL RESOURCES

Draw/fill in the blanks

STATE CAPITAL: ______________________

STATE FLAG

REGION

- ○ Northeast
- ○ Southwest
- ○ West
- ○ Midwest
- ○ Southeast

STATE BIRD

____

STATE FLOWER

____

COLOR IN THE STATE ON THE MAP BELOW

ONE LANDMARK

AN INTERESTING FACT

NATURAL RESOURCES

Draw/fill in the blanks

STATE CAPITAL: ______________________

STATE FLAG

REGION

- ◯ Northeast
- ◯ Southwest
- ◯ West
- ◯ Midwest
- ◯ Southeast

STATE BIRD

____

STATE FLOWER

____

COLOR IN THE STATE ON THE MAP BELOW

ONE LANDMARK

AN INTERESTING FACT

NATURAL RESOURCES

Draw/fill in the blanks

STATE CAPITAL: ______________________________

STATE FLAG

REGION

- ◯ Northeast
- ◯ Southwest
- ◯ West
- ◯ Midwest
- ◯ Southeast

STATE BIRD

____

STATE FLOWER

____

COLOR IN THE STATE ON THE MAP BELOW

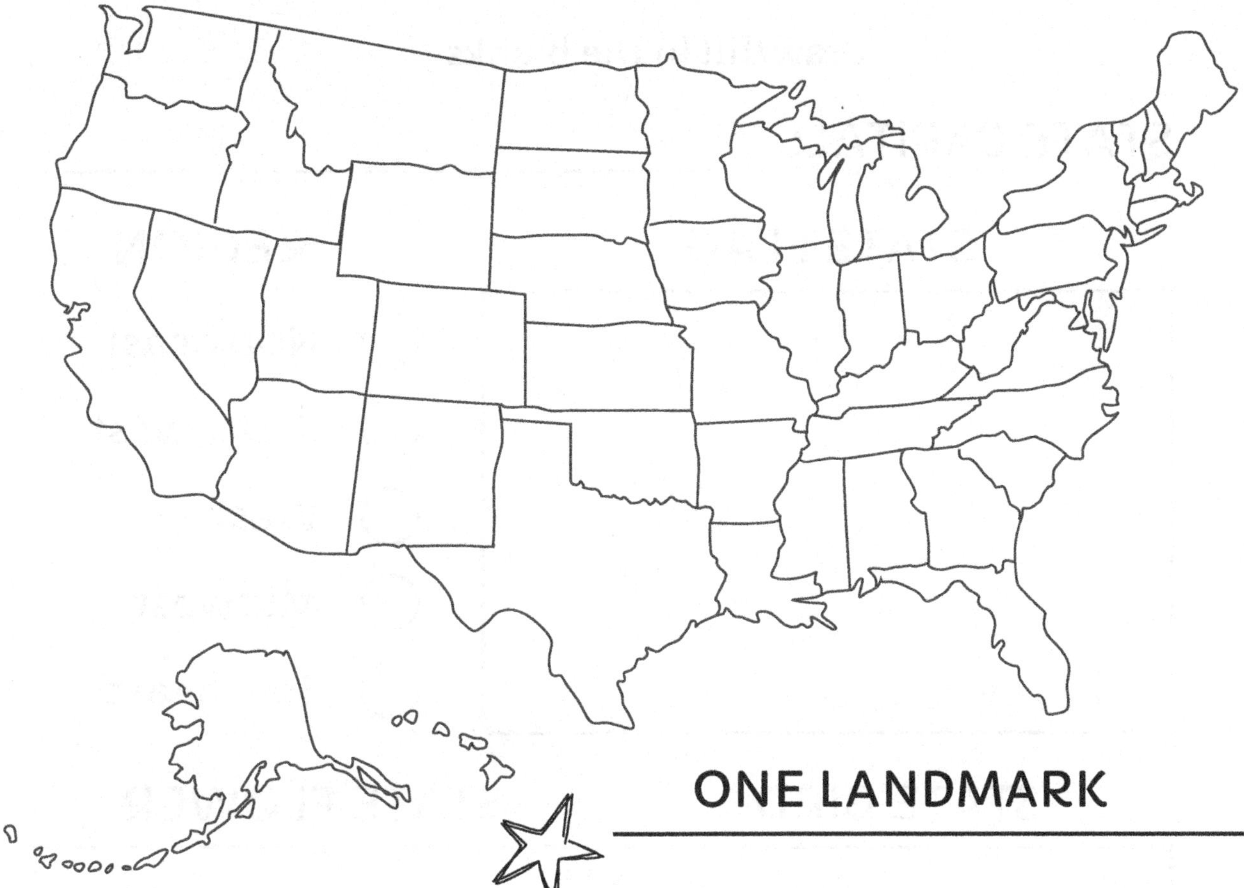

ONE LANDMARK

AN INTERESTING FACT

Draw/fill in the blanks

STATE CAPITAL: ______________________

STATE FLAG

REGION

- Northeast
- Southwest
- West
- Midwest
- Southeast

STATE BIRD

____

STATE FLOWER

____

COLOR IN THE STATE ON THE MAP BELOW

ONE LANDMARK

AN INTERESTING FACT

NATURAL RESOURCES

Draw/fill in the blanks

STATE CAPITAL: ______________________

STATE FLAG

REGION

- Northeast
- Southwest
- West
- Midwest
- Southeast

STATE BIRD

____

STATE FLOWER

____

COLOR IN THE STATE ON THE MAP BELOW

ONE LANDMARK

AN INTERESTING FACT

NATURAL RESOURCES

Draw/fill in the blanks

STATE CAPITAL: ______________________

STATE FLAG

REGION

- ◯ Northeast
- ◯ Southwest
- ◯ West
- ◯ Midwest
- ◯ Southeast

STATE BIRD

____

STATE FLOWER

____

COLOR IN THE STATE ON THE MAP BELOW

ONE LANDMARK

AN INTERESTING FACT

NATURAL RESOURCES

Draw/fill in the blanks

STATE CAPITAL: ______________________________

STATE FLAG

REGION

- ◯ Northeast
- ◯ Southwest
- ◯ West
- ◯ Midwest
- ◯ Southeast

STATE BIRD

____

STATE FLOWER

____

COLOR IN THE STATE ON THE MAP BELOW

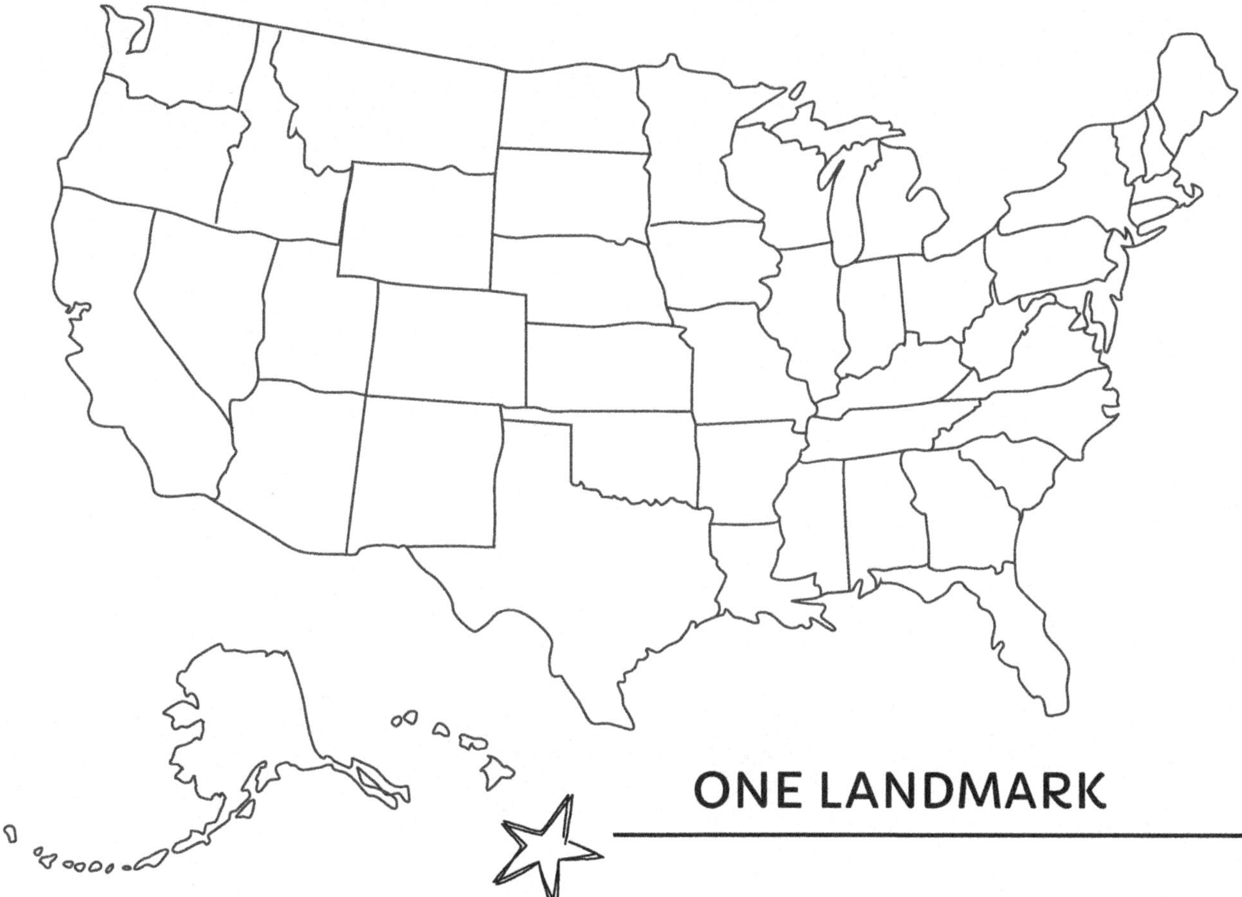

ONE LANDMARK

AN INTERESTING FACT

Made in the USA
Monee, IL
14 August 2025

23196936R00057